RECIPE OF THE WEEK ·· ICE CREAM ··

ICE CREAM

52 EASY RECIPES FOR YEAR-ROUND FROZEN TREATS

SALLY SAMPSON

PHOTOGRAPHY BY ALEXANDRA GRABLEWSKI

WILEY

JOHN WILEY & SONS, INC.

PHOTOGRAPHY COPYRIGHT © 2008 BY ALEXANDRA GRABLEWSKI
BOOK DESIGN BY DEBORAH KERNER
FOOD STYLING BY BRIAN PRESTON-CAMPBELL
PROP STYLING BY LESLIE SIEGEL

Library of Congress Cataloging-in-Publication Data:
Sampson, Sally, 1955-
    Recipe of the week : ice cream / Sally Sampson ; photography by Yunhee Kim.
        p. cm.
    Includes index.
    ISBN: 978-0-470-16945-2 (paper)
    1. Ice cream, ices, etc. I. Title
    TX795.S36 2008
    641.8'62—dc22

                                    2008009577

Printed in China
10 9 8 7 6 5 4 3 2

For Ben and Lauren,
who prefer a nice piece
of fruit. Well, usually.

Contents

Acknowledgments

I began work on this cookbook as someone wedded only to coffee and burnt caramel ice cream. I didn't wander far and was, therefore, in need of much inspiration, particularly since Justin, my editor, didn't want a book filled with recipes you could get anywhere: he wanted interesting, unusual and, if commonplace, the absolute best version.

Gus Rancatore, the maestro behind Toscanini's Ice Cream, unquestionably the best ice cream around Boston, gave me a crash course in ice cream making. I couldn't have done a thing without his help.

Literally everyone I know (you know who you are) gave me ideas. Of course, Justin pushed me and Carla and Jenny were, as always, indispensable.

The publisher thanks Cuisinart for their kind donation of a Cuisinart Supreme™ Commercial Quality Ice Cream Maker (Model # ICE-50BC) for use in making the ice creams for the photography.

If you want to **become really popular**—with housepainters, teachers, small children, teenagers, friends, random adults—really with just about anyone, even people who barely like you, my suggestion is to write a book on ice cream and be very generous with what you produce.

If truth be told, I was generous, in part, because I wanted feedback (even negative) and I didn't want a freezer overflowing with more and more ice cream. Additionally, homemade ice cream is really at its peak when it's just been made (or within a few hours): after a day, the texture loses its vibrancy.

I approached writing a book about ice cream more scientifically than I had any other food group. I played with temperature and found that there is no point in rushing things: temperature matters. When I say a mixture must be 40°F, I mean it, and although I recommend one of those small pocket thermometers that you often see sticking of out chef's coats, I don't have absolute faith in them. If you have any doubt whether something is cold enough, add another hour. On the other hand, I played endlessly with the quantity of sugar, fruit and the proportion of cream to milk. As a rule the ice creams in this book are **lower in sugar** (it's fine to increase if you want), **higher in flavor** (the peach ice cream has a massive amount of fresh peach in it) and **lower in fat** than most commercial ice creams. When you make ice cream with too much heavy cream or too many eggs, you coat your taste buds and as a result, dull them. And then, what's the point?

Toasting Nuts & Coconut

Preheat the oven to 350°F. Place the nuts/coconut on a baking sheet or in a shallow pan, transfer to the oven and bake until lightly colored and fragrant, about 10 minutes.

Set aside to cool.

Sugar Syrup

The few recipes that are eggless call for sugar syrup, which can sit in the fridge for a full month: I like sugar syrup because it eliminates the step of dissolving the sugar and therefore also the time for cooling. It is particularly nice for those who are impatient.

Place 1 cup white sugar and 1 cup water in a small saucepan and cook, over medium high heat, until the sugar has completely dissolved, about 3 minutes. Set aside to cool, cover and refrigerate up to 1 month.

the recipes

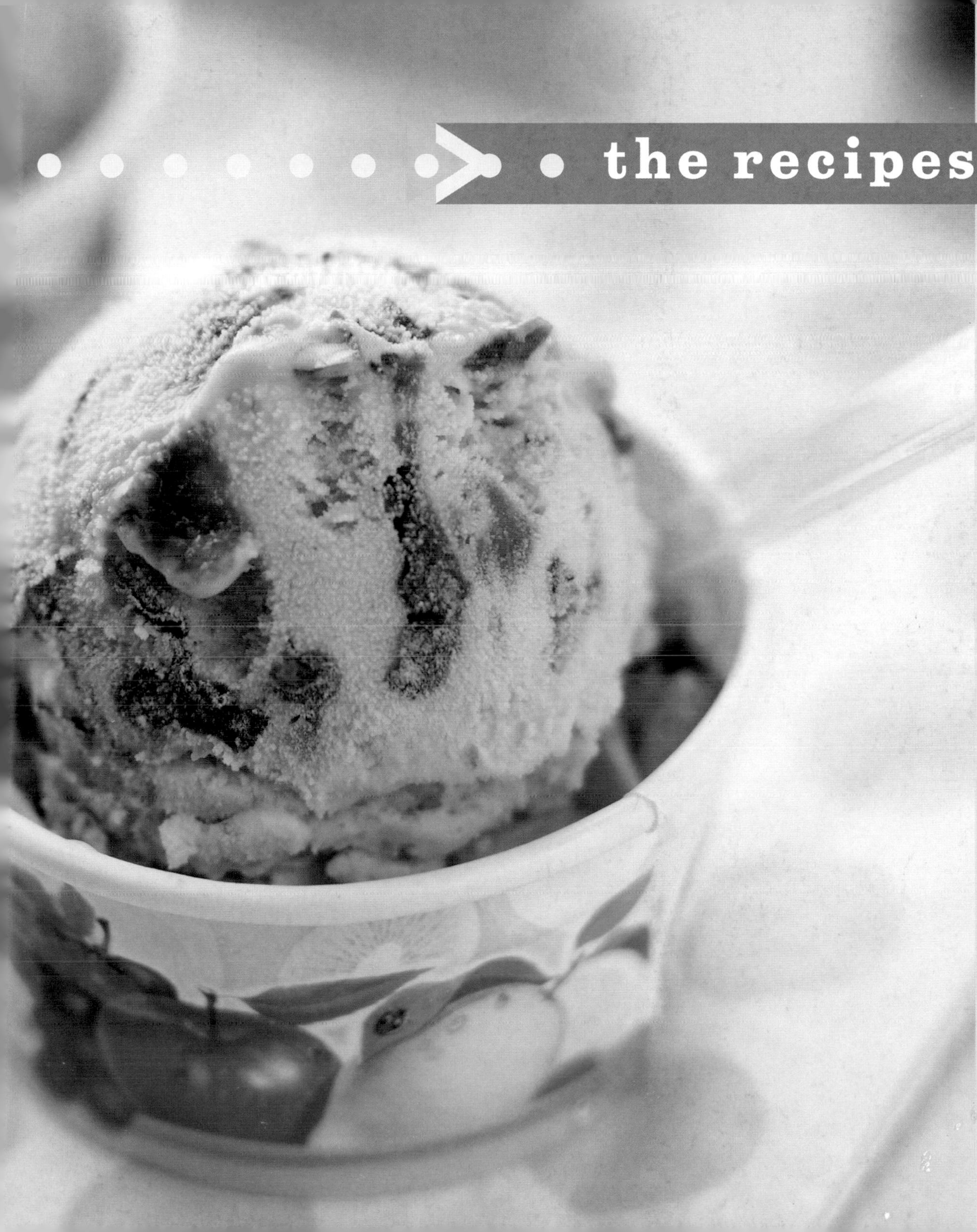

Sweet Cream

Generally speaking, sweet cream is the foundation for all ice cream flavors that include mix-ins. One of the most popular flavors, it is a must-have in your ice cream repertoire and the ideal substitute for whipped cream on almost any kind of cake. My favorite mix-ins include chocolate cake, carrot cake, broken cookies, pieces of brownies, mini M&M's ®, banana bread, etc. Add about 1 cup mix-ins during the last 5 minutes of churning.

1 ½ cups whole milk

1 ½ cups heavy cream

¼ cup sugar syrup (see page xiii)

or white sugar

If using sugar syrup: Place the milk, cream and sugar syrup in a bowl and whisk well. Transfer to an ice cream maker and proceed according to the manufacturer's instructions.

If using sugar: Place the milk, cream and sugar in a medium size pan and cook, stirring well, over low heat until the sugar dissolves, about 3 minutes. Set aside to cool to room temperature. Cover and refrigerate until the mixture reaches 40°F, about 2 hours, and then transfer to an ice cream maker and proceed according to the manufacturer's instructions.

Vanilla Ice Cream with Bittersweet Cocoa Sauce

MAKES 1 ½ TO 2 PINTS

Nearly all recipes for vanilla ice cream call for either vanilla beans or vanilla extract. Vanilla extract is made by extracting the flavor from vanilla beans in an alcoholic solution and thus its flavor is more dilute than the delicate yet strong flavor that comes from the seeds inside vanilla pods. The finest vanilla ice cream utilizes both but since vanilla beans are fantastically expensive, they are rarely found in most commercial ice creams.

FOR THE ICE CREAM:

1 ½ cups whole milk

½ cup white sugar or sugar syrup (see page xiii)

One 4-inch vanilla bean, split and scraped

1 ½ cups heavy cream

1 teaspoon vanilla extract

Pinch kosher salt

FOR THE BITTERSWEET COCOA SAUCE:

¼ cup unsweetened cocoa powder

1 cup heavy cream

1 to 2 tablespoons white sugar

To make the ice cream: If using sugar: Place ½ cup of the milk, the sugar and vanilla bean seeds and pod in a medium size pan and cook over low heat. Set aside to cool to room temperature. Add the remaining 1 cup milk, the cream, vanilla extract and salt and whisk to combine. Cover and refrigerate until the mixture reaches 40°F, about 1 hour. Remove the vanilla bean. Transfer to an ice cream maker and proceed according to the manufacturer's instructions.

If using sugar syrup: Place all the ingredients in a bowl and mix well. Cover and refrigerate until the mixture reaches 40°F, about 20 minutes. Remove the vanilla bean. Transfer to an ice cream maker and proceed according to the manufacturer's instructions.

To make the bittersweet cocoa sauce: Place the cocoa, cream and sugar in a small saucepan and bring to low boil over medium heat. Cook, whisking constantly, until it just begins to thicken, about 10 minutes. Serve hot, cold or at room temperature.

Dried Plum Gelato

Gelato, from the Italian word for frozen, is the Italian version of ice cream. More about depth of flavor and less about the mouth-feel of fat, gelato tends to have a creamier and richer texture than American ice cream and yet has a lower fat content. Almost all ice cream can be adjusted to become gelato: simply make the ratio of milk to cream 2:1 instead of 1:1. You can also try this gelato by substituting dried figs, apricots or dates for the plums. Garnish with currants or lightly toasted almonds or walnuts.

1 cup dried plums, finely chopped	⅔ cup white sugar
½ cup boiling water	4 large egg yolks, at room temperature
2 cups whole milk	1 tablespoon Armagnac
1 cup heavy cream	Pinch kosher salt

Place the plums and boiling water in a small bowl and set aside for 30 minutes.

Place the milk, cream and ⅓ cup of the sugar in a small pan and cook over low heat, whisking from time to time, until it is warm, about 175°F.

Place the egg yolks, ⅓ cup of the sugar, the Armagnac and salt in a small metal bowl and whisk until completely mixed. Add ¼ cup of the warm milk mixture to the eggs, whisking all the while. Continue adding the milk mixture to the eggs, ¼ cup at a time, until you have added about 1½ cups. Slowly, whisking all the while, return the milk and egg mixture to the remaining milk mixture in the pan and continue cooking until it just begins to thicken or reaches about 185°F. Do not allow the mixture to boil. Pour through a medium fine strainer into a metal bowl, discard the solids and set aside until it reaches room temperature. Add the plum mixture, mix well, cover and refrigerate at least 8 hours or overnight. Transfer to an ice cream maker and proceed according to the manufacturer's instructions.

Cocoa Sorbet

One of the greatest qualities of cocoa sorbet is that you would swear it was filled with all sorts of high fat ingredients and yet it is not. To me, cocoa powder (the cocoa solids that remain after the cocoa butter has been extracted, and then dried, processed and often "dutched") offers a texture and depth of flavor that is often superior to what you get from chocolate.

2 cups unsweetened cocoa powder

2 cups sugar syrup (see page xiii)

1 teaspoon vanilla extract

Place the cocoa powder, sugar syrup and vanilla extract in a blender and blend until the cocoa powder has dissolved. Cover and refrigerate until the mixture reaches 40°F, about 1 hour. Transfer to an ice cream maker and proceed according to the manufacturer's instructions.

French Vanilla Ice Cream with Caramel Sauce

Most high-end ice cream shops sell both vanilla and French vanilla ice cream, yet few people actually know the difference. French vanilla refers to the French style of making ice cream, which consists of vanilla pods, cream and egg yolks. Conversely, vanilla ice cream generally consists of just vanilla pods and cream, without the egg yolks. French vanilla ice cream is yellower and has a much richer flavor and a heavier texture.

This recipe calls for less sugar and fewer eggs than most French vanilla recipes. To me, it is about as sweet and rich as I could want. Great with Burnt Caramel Sauce (see page 72) or fresh berries.

FOR THE ICE CREAM:

1 ½ cups whole milk

1 ½ cups heavy cream

½ cup white sugar

One 4-inch vanilla bean, split and scraped

4 large egg yolks, at room temperature

1 teaspoon vanilla extract

Pinch kosher salt

FOR THE CARAMEL SAUCE:

1 cup heavy cream

½ cup brown sugar

½ teaspoon vanilla extract

1 tablespoon unsalted butter, at room temperature

To make the ice cream: Place the milk, cream, ¼ cup of the sugar and the vanilla bean seeds and pod (now empty) in a small pan and cook over low heat, whisking from time to time, until it is warm, about 175°F.

Place the egg yolks, ¼ cup of the sugar, the vanilla extract and salt in a small metal bowl and whisk until completely mixed. Add ¼ cup of the warm milk mixture to the eggs, whisking all the while. Continue adding the milk mixture to the eggs, ¼ cup at a time, until you have added about 1½ cups. Slowly, whisking all the while, return the now milk and egg mixture to the remaining milk mixture in the pan and continue cooking until it just begins to thicken or reaches about 185°F. Do not allow the

continued on next page

mixture to boil. Strain into a metal bowl and discard the solids. Set the mixture aside until it reaches room temperature.

Cover and refrigerate until it reaches 40°F, about 3 hours. Transfer to an ice cream maker and proceed according to the manufacturer's instructions.

To make the caramel sauce: Place the cream in a small pot over high heat and cook until it is just scalded (starting to bubble around the edges of the pot). Place the brown sugar in another pot and cook, stirring, until it just begins to darken, about 3 minutes. Very gradually, add the cream to the brown sugar and, using a whisk, combine until smooth. Add the vanilla extract and butter and whisk again. Serve hot or at room temperature.

Pretzel and Chocolate Gelato

My friend Margery Galen suggested this combo to me, after having tried—and loved—it at an ice cream shop in Alaska. Anyone who likes the contrast of salty and sweet will love this gelato. Margery's original suggestion was for chocolate-covered pretzels but I use pretzels and chocolate chips simply because they are more likely to be on hand.

2 cups whole milk

1 cup heavy cream

½ cup white sugar

4 large egg yolks, at room temperature

1 teaspoon vanilla extract

½ cup crushed salted pretzels

½ cup chopped semi sweet chocolate chips

Place the milk, cream and ¼ cup of the sugar in a small pan and cook over low heat, whisking from time to time, until it is warm, about 175°F.

Place the egg yolks, ¼ cup of the sugar and the vanilla extract in a small metal bowl and whisk until completely mixed. Add ¼ cup of the warm milk mixture to the eggs, whisking all the while. Continue adding milk to the eggs, ¼ cup at a time, until you have added about 1½ cups. Slowly, whisking all the while, return the now milk and egg mixture to the remaining milk mixture in the pan and continue cooking until it just begins to thicken or reaches about 185°F. Do not allow the mixture to boil. Strain into a metal bowl, discard the solids and set aside until it reaches room temperature.

Cover and refrigerate until it reaches 40°F, about 3 hours. Transfer to an ice cream maker and proceed according to the manufacturer's instructions.

When the ice cream is just beginning to come together but has not hardened completely, add the pretzels and chocolate chips and process for about 5 more minutes.

Banana Sorbet

Bananas, the most popular tropical fruit in the US, make the texture of this sorbet feel just like ice cream. Be absolutely sure to use overripe bananas: in fact, the funkier the better!

2 cups pureed overripe bananas

1 cup sugar syrup (see page xiii)

1 tablespoon fresh lemon or lime juice

Place the bananas, sugar syrup and lemon juice in a blender or food processor and blend until smooth. Cover and refrigerate until the mixture reaches 40°F, about 2 hours.

Transfer to an ice cream maker and proceed according to the manufacturer's instructions.

Graham Cracker Malted Vanilla Ice Cream

MAKES 1 ½ TO 2 PINTS

I am a huge fan of malt (a powder made from dried whole milk, malted barley and wheat flour) and think it's a great addition to most ice cream flavors: banana, strawberry and chocolate, among them. Malt (aka malted milk powder) is sold in most grocery stores and is well loved for its use in a popular milkshake flavor made from vanilla ice cream, whole milk and a scoop of malt powder.

Serve with roasted plums or apricots or garnish with chocolate chips, toasted or fresh coconut or tiny marshmallows.

1 ½ cups whole milk	1 teaspoon vanilla extract
1 ½ cups heavy cream	Pinch kosher salt
½ cup white sugar	⅓ cup malt powder
One 4-inch vanilla bean, split and scraped (optional)	3 graham crackers (plain, cinnamon or chocolate covered), crumbled
3 large egg yolks, at room temperature	

Place the milk, cream, ¼ cup of the sugar and, if desired, the vanilla bean seeds and pod (now empty) in a small pan and cook over low heat, whisking from time to time, until it is warm, about 175°F.

Place the egg yolks, ¼ cup of the sugar, the vanilla extract and salt in a small metal bowl and whisk until completely mixed. Add ¼ cup of the warm milk mixture to the eggs, whisking all the while. Continue adding the milk to the eggs, ¼ cup at a time, until you have added about 1½ cups. Slowly, whisking all the while, return the now milk and egg mixture to the remaining milk mixture in the pan and continue cooking until it just begins to thicken or reaches about 185°F. Do not allow the mixture to boil. Strain into a metal bowl and discard the solids. Gradually add the malt powder, whisking all the while. Set the mixture aside until it reaches room temperature.

continued on page 14

Cover and refrigerate until it reaches 40°F, about 3 hours. Transfer to an ice cream maker and proceed according to the manufacturer's instructions.

When the ice cream is just beginning to come together but has not hardened completely, add the graham crackers and process for about 5 more minutes.

Lemon Vanilla Ice Cream with Raspberry Sauce

MAKES 1 ½ TO 2 PINTS

At first blush, the combination of the strong lemon flavor and the lush dairy seems odd, but the lemon brightens the vanilla extract and makes it all the more intense.

FOR THE ICE CREAM:

½ cup white sugar

¼ cup fresh lemon juice

1½ cups whole milk

1½ cups heavy cream

One 4-inch vanilla bean, split and scraped

4 large egg yolks, at room temperature

1 teaspoon vanilla extract

Pinch kosher salt

Zest of 1 lemon

FOR THE RASPBERRY SAUCE:

2 pints fresh raspberries

½ cup white sugar

To make the ice cream: Place the sugar and lemon juice in a small pan and bring to a boil. Remove from the heat and set aside for 10 minutes. Cover and refrigerate until called for in recipe.

Place the milk, cream and vanilla bean seeds and pod (now empty) in a small pan and cook over low heat, whisking from time to time, until it is warm, about 175°F.

Place the egg yolks, vanilla extract and salt in a small metal bowl and whisk until completely mixed. Add ¼ cup of the warm milk mixture to the eggs, whisking all the while. Continue adding milk to the eggs, ¼ cup at a time, until you have added about 1½ cups. Slowly, whisking all the while, return the now milk and egg mixture to the remaining milk mixture in the pan and continue cooking until it just begins to thicken or reaches about 185°F. Do not allow the mixture to boil. Strain into a metal bowl, discard the solids and set aside until it reaches room temperature.

Cover and refrigerate until it reaches 40°F, about 3 hours. Add the sugar lemon mixture and the lemon zest and whisk to combine. Transfer to an ice cream maker and proceed according to the manufacturer's instructions.

To make the raspberry sauce: Place the raspberries and sugar in a small saucepan and bring to a boil, stirring occasionally, over high heat. Cook until the sugar has dissolved. Serve at room temperature or chilled.

Annette's Crunchy Coffee Ice Cream

MAKES 1 ½ TO 2 PINTS

My sister-in-law Annette loves to drink coffee but doesn't like coffee ice cream unless it's made using coffee grounds: as long as you like the grittiness of the ground coffee (which I do), you'll love her version. Although Annette is a purist, I like to add Heath bars, coarsely chopped toasted almonds, chocolate chips or Oreos.

1 ½ cups whole milk

1 ½ cups heavy cream

½ cup white sugar

3 large egg yolks, at room temperature

1 teaspoon vanilla extract

¼ cup coarsely ground coffee beans

Place the milk, cream and ¼ cup of the sugar in a small pan and cook over low heat, whisking from time to time, until it is warm, about 175°F.

Place the egg yolks, ¼ cup of the sugar and the vanilla extract in a small metal bowl and whisk until completely mixed. Add ¼ cup of the warm milk mixture to the eggs, whisking all the while. Continue adding the milk mixture to the eggs, ¼ cup at a time, until you have added about 1½ cups. Slowly, whisking all the while, return the now milk and egg mixture to the remaining milk mixture in the pan and continue cooking until it just begins to thicken or reaches about 185°F. Do not allow the mixture to boil. Strain into a metal bowl, discard the solids and set aside until it reaches room temperature.

Cover and refrigerate until it reaches 40°F, about 3 hours. Add the ground coffee and whisk until combined. Transfer to an ice cream maker and proceed according to the manufacturer's instructions.

Balsamic and Black Pepper Gelato

The classic Italian combination of balsamic vinegar and black pepper is most commonly found drizzled on meats or fruits, especially peaches and strawberries. Although black pepper adds pungency to savory dishes, when added to the sweet creamy ice cream flavor, its flavor is far more subdued. Serve with fresh or roasted peaches and/or fresh strawberries.

2 cups whole milk

1 cup heavy cream

½ cup white sugar

3 large egg yolks, at room temperature

1 teaspoon vanilla extract

1 tablespoon freshly cracked black pepper

1 tablespoon balsamic vinegar

Place the milk, cream and ¼ cup of the sugar in a small pan and cook over low heat, whisking from time to time, until it is warm, about 175°F.

Place the egg yolks, ¼ cup of the sugar and the vanilla extract in a small metal bowl and whisk until completely mixed. Add ¼ cup of the warm milk mixture to the eggs, whisking all the while. Continue adding the milk mixture to the eggs, ¼ cup at a time, until you have added about 1½ cups. Slowly, whisking all the while, return the now milk and egg mixture to the remaining milk mixture in the pan and continue cooking until it just begins to thicken or reaches about 185°F. Do not allow the mixture to boil. Strain into a metal bowl, discard the solids and set aside until it reaches room temperature. Add the pepper and balsamic vinegar and whisk until combined.

Cover and refrigerate until it reaches 40°F, about 3 hours. Transfer to an ice cream maker and proceed according to the manufacturer's instructions.

Fresh Fig Gelato with Orange and Cinnamon

MAKES 1 ½ TO 2 PINTS

I had never had fig ice cream but when I walked by a gorgeous cascading display, the piles of fresh figs beckoned. The delicate taste is sweet and truly sublime, the texture slightly smooth yet chewy with tiny crackles of crunch. If you like, you can drizzle a little bit of honey on top.

1 pound fresh figs, chopped

¼ cup fresh orange juice

1 tablespoon plus ½ cup light brown sugar

¼ teaspoon ground cinnamon

2 cups whole milk

1 cup heavy cream

3 large egg yolks, at room temperature

½ teaspoon vanilla extract

Pinch kosher salt

Place the figs, orange juice, 1 tablespoon of the brown sugar and the cinnamon in a small pan and cook over low heat until the figs have softened, 10 to 15 minutes, depending on the thickness of the skin. Mash until the mixture is almost pureed but still has some texture and set aside until it reaches room temperature. Cover and refrigerate.

In the meantime, place the milk, cream and ¼ cup of the brown sugar in a small pan and cook over low heat, whisking from time to time, until it is warm, about 175°F.

Place the egg yolks, ¼ cup of the brown sugar, vanilla extract and salt in a small metal bowl and whisk until completely mixed. Add ¼ cup of the warm milk mixture to the eggs, whisking all the while. Continue adding milk to the eggs, ¼ cup at a time, until you have added about 1½ cups. Slowly, whisking all the while, return the now milk and egg mixture to the remaining milk mixture in the pan and continue cooking until it just begins to thicken or reaches about 185°F. Do not allow the mixture to boil. Pour through a medium fine strainer into a metal bowl, discard the solids and set aside until it reaches room temperature.

Add the cooled fig mixture, cover and refrigerate until it reaches 40°F, about 3 hours. Transfer to an ice cream maker and proceed according to the manufacturer's instructions.

18

Saffron Ice Cream

MAKES 1 ½ TO 2 PINTS

Due to the exorbitant cost of saffron threads, saffron ice cream—creamy, almost citrus-y, almost bitter and vibrantly colored—is outrageously expensive to make but well worth the occasional splurge. Although saffron ice cream is often available at Indian restaurants, saffron is primarily known for its use in French bouillabaisse, Italian risotto and Spanish paella.

3 cups half and half

½ cup white sugar

½ teaspoon saffron threads (or ¼ teaspoon saffron and ¼ teaspoon cardamom)

4 large egg yolks, at room temperature

Pinch kosher salt

Place the half and half, ¼ cup of the sugar and the saffron in a small pan and cook over low heat, whisking from time to time, until it is warm, about 175°F.

Place the egg yolks, ¼ cup of the sugar and the salt in a small metal bowl and whisk until completely mixed. Add ¼ cup of the warm half and half mixture to the eggs, whisking all the while. Continue adding half and half to the eggs, ¼ cup at a time, until you have added about 1½ cups. Slowly, whisking all the while, return the now half and half and egg mixture to the remaining half and half mixture in the pan and continue cooking until it just begins to thicken or reaches about 185°F. Do not allow the mixture to boil. Pour through a medium fine strainer into a metal bowl, discard the solids and set aside until it reaches room temperature.

Cover and refrigerate at least 8 hours or overnight. Transfer to an ice cream maker and proceed according to the manufacturer's instructions.

Orange Granita

What I love about this easy to make Orange Granita is that its ingredients are always on hand in my house. Though it's a light and refreshing dessert, it's also wonderful as a palate cleanser between meals. Grapefruit and tangerine juices are ready substitutes.

4 cups fresh orange juice
1 cup white sugar

Place the juice and sugar in a shallow pan and mix until the sugar has dissolved. Transfer to the freezer. Using a fork, stir every 15 minutes until frozen, about 2 hours.

Apricot Raspberry Sorbet

MAKES 1 1/2 TO 2 PINTS

For me it's almost a waste to use melt-in-your-mouth fresh raspberries as an ingredient (because they are so amazing eaten solo) but I make an exception for this delicate sorbet. Here the raspberry tartness melds perfectly with the slightly musky apricot.

2 cups apricot juice

1 cup raspberries (frozen or fresh)

2 tablespoons sugar syrup (see page xiii)

2 teaspoons vodka

2 teaspoon vanilla extract

Place the apricot juice, raspberries and syrup in a blender or food processor and blend until smooth. Cover and refrigerate until the mixture reaches 40°F, about 20 minutes. Add the vodka and vanilla extract and stir well. Transfer to an ice cream maker and proceed according to the manufacturer's instructions.

Egg Nog Ice Cream

MAKES 1 ½ TO 2 PINTS

Mostly associated with Christmas and New Year's, eggnog, traditionally made from milk, sugar, cream, eggs, nutmeg and sometimes liquor, is a beverage people tend to either love or loathe: I don't know anyone in between. Even if you aren't a fan, try this very adult ice cream: for me, the flavors work even better in the ice cream than in the drink.

3 cups half and half	8 large egg yolks, at room temperature
½ cup white sugar	Pinch kosher salt
½ teaspoon freshly grated nutmeg	2 tablespoons Amaretto
Zest of 1 lemon	2 tablespoons Anisette or Sambuca
Zest of 1 orange	2 tablespoons Grand Marnier, Triple Sec or
One 4-inch vanilla bean, split and scraped	Cointreau

Place the half and half, ¼ cup of the sugar, the nutmeg, lemon zest, orange zest and vanilla bean seeds and pod (now empty) in a small pan and cook over low heat, whisking from time to time, until it is warm, about 175°F.

Place the egg yolks, ¼ cup of the sugar and the salt in a small metal bowl and whisk until completely mixed. Add ¼ cup of the warm half and half mixture to the eggs, whisking all the while. Continue adding half and half to the eggs, ¼ cup at a time, until you have added about 1½ cups. Slowly, whisking all the while, return the now half and half and egg mixture to the remaining half and half mixture in the pan and continue cooking until it just begins to thicken or reaches about 185°F. Do not allow the mixture to boil. Pour through a medium fine strainer into a metal bowl, discard the solids and set aside until it reaches room temperature.

Add the Amaretto, Anisette and Grand Marnier and stir well. Cover and refrigerate at least 8 hours or overnight. Transfer to an ice cream maker and proceed according to the manufacturer's instructions.

Cardamom Ice Cream

Although it is in the ginger family, cardamom (kardamomma in Iceland) is one of the most difficult flavors to describe. It has a very distinct flavor, doesn't really taste like anything else and yet it is reminiscent of many things, since it is often paired with so many other spices and flavors. It is used as an ingredient in foods as disparate as cookies, curries, pickles and coffee. Garnish with chopped toasted almonds, pistachios and/or shortbread cookies.

2 cups half and half

1 cup sweetened condensed milk

4 tablespoons white sugar

1 tablespoon freshly ground cardamom seeds

4 large egg yolks, at room temperature

1 teaspoon vanilla extract

Pinch kosher salt

Place the half and half, condensed milk, 2 tablespoons of the sugar and the cardamom in a small pan and cook over low heat, whisking from time to time, until it is warm, about 175°F.

Place the egg yolks, 2 tablespoons sugar, vanilla extract and salt in a small metal bowl and whisk until completely mixed. Add ¼ cup of the warm half and half mixture to the eggs, whisking all the while. Continue adding the half and half mixture to the eggs, ¼ cup at a time, until you have added about 1½ cups. Slowly, whisking all the while, return the now half and half and egg mixture to the remaining half and half mixture in the pan and continue cooking until it just begins to thicken or reaches about 185°F. Do not allow the mixture to boil. Strain into a metal bowl, discard the solids and set aside until it reaches room temperature.

Cover and refrigerate at least 8 hours or overnight. Transfer to an ice cream maker and proceed according to the manufacturer's instructions.

Coffee Granita

MAKES 1 1/2 TO 2 PINTS

Another Italian semi-frozen dessert, granita does not require any special equipment and is effortless to set up with ingredients you are likely to have on hand. Unlike sorbet, which has similar ingredients, granita is grainy in texture. Serve with a big dollop of fresh whipped cream: skip the canned stuff and make the real thing!

3 3/4 cups hot brewed espresso or strong coffee
3/4 cup white sugar

Place the coffee and sugar in a shallow pan and mix until the sugar has dissolved. Set the mixture aside until it reaches room temperature. Transfer to the freezer. Using a fork, stir every 15 minutes until frozen, about 2 hours.

Peanut Butter Chocolate Chip Ice Cream

MAKES 1 ½ TO 2 PINTS

A classic combo requested by thirteen-year-old Charlie Steinberg. Instead of using peanut butter ice cream and adding chocolate chips, we used a variation of vanilla ice cream, added big gobs of peanut butter and laced it with chocolate chips.

1 ½ cups whole milk

1 ½ cups heavy cream

½ cup white sugar

2 large egg yolks, at room temperature

1 teaspoon vanilla extract

¾ cup mini semi-sweet chocolate chips

⅔ cup peanut butter

Place the milk, cream and ¼ cup of the sugar in a small pan and cook over low heat, whisking from time to time, until it is warm, about 175°F.

Place the egg yolks, ¼ cup of the sugar and the vanilla extract in a small metal bowl and whisk until completely mixed. Add ¼ cup of the warm milk mixture to the eggs, whisking all the while. Continue adding milk to the eggs, ¼ cup at a time, until you have added about 1½ cups. Slowly, whisking all the while, return the now milk and egg mixture to the remaining milk mixture in the pan and continue cooking until it just begins to thicken or reaches about 185°F. Do not allow the mixture to boil. Pour through a medium fine strainer into a metal bowl, discard the solids and set aside until it reaches room temperature.

Cover and refrigerate until it reaches 40°F, about 3 hours. Transfer to an ice cream maker and proceed according to the manufacturer's instructions.

When the ice cream is just beginning to come together but has not hardened completely, add the chocolate chips and process for about 4 more minutes. Add the peanut butter, in 1 tablespoon gobs. Do not allow the peanut butter to be incorporated into the ice cream.

Grapefruit Sorbet

MAKES 1 1/2 TO 2 PINTS

It is essential that you use freshly squeezed grapefruit juice for this tangy sorbet. There is nothing quite like it! If you can't make it, or buy it, make a different sorbet! For an even more adult version, add 1 teaspoon white or black pepper.

3 cups fresh grapefruit juice

¾ cup light brown sugar

1 ½ tablespoons citron vodka

Place the grapefruit juice and brown sugar in a bowl and whisk until the brown sugar has dissolved. Set aside until it reaches room temperature. Add the vodka and stir well. Cover and refrigerate until the mixture reaches 40°F, about 1 hour. Transfer to an ice cream maker and proceed according to the manufacturer's instructions.

Dark Chocolate Ice Cream

MAKES 1½ TO 2 PINTS

Jean Anthelme Brillat-Savarin, the famous gastronome from the 1700s, said: "Those who have been too long . . . at their labor, who have drunk too long at the cup of voluptuousness, who feel they have become temporarily inhumane, who are tormented by their families, who find life sad and love ephemeral; they should all eat chocolate and they will be comforted." I think he was referring to this black, deep dark chocolate ice cream. The list of ingredients to add in the beginning (gingerroot, malt, mint, coconut, pepper, cayenne, chipotle, cinnamon, Earl Grey tea and ground coffee) is rivaled in length only by the list you can add during the last five minutes: toasted almonds, pistachios, walnuts, hazelnuts, pecans, bananas, dried or fresh cherries and on and on . . .

1½ cups whole milk	2 tablespoons white sugar
1½ cups heavy cream	1 teaspoon vanilla extract
8 ounces semi-sweet chocolate	Pinch kosher salt
3 large egg yolks, at room temperature	¼ cup Cointreau or Grand Marnier (optional)

Place the milk, cream and chocolate in a small pan and cook over low heat, whisking from time to time, until it is warm, about 175°F.

Place the egg yolks, sugar, vanilla extract and salt in a small metal bowl and whisk until completely mixed. Add ¼ cup of the warm milk mixture to the eggs, whisking all the while. Continue adding milk to the eggs, ¼ cup at a time, until you have added about 1½ cups. Slowly, whisking all the while, return the now milk and egg mixture to the remaining milk mixture in the pan and continue cooking until it just begins to thicken or reaches about 185°F. Do not allow the mixture to boil. Pour through a medium fine strainer into a metal bowl, discard the solids and set aside until it reaches room temperature.

Cover and refrigerate until it reaches 40°F, about 3 hours. Add the Cointreau, if desired. Transfer to an ice cream maker and proceed according to the manufacturer's instructions.

Pomegranate Sorbet

Pomegranates, also called Chinese apples, show up everywhere now on the menus of hip restaurants, in school box lunches, in every juice permutation you can think of. Their sweet-tart flavor is a perfect match for all the citrus in this sorbet. Enjoy between courses or after a meal.

3 cups pomegranate juice

¾ cup fresh grapefruit juice

⅓ cup white sugar

2 tablespoons fresh lime or lemon juice

1 tablespoon finely grated grapefruit zest (optional)

Place the pomegranate and grapefruit juices and the sugar in a bowl and whisk until the sugar has dissolved. Add the lime juice and grapefruit zest, if desired, and stir well. Cover and refrigerate until the mixture reaches 40°F. Transfer to an ice cream maker and proceed according to the manufacturer's instructions.

Rocky Road Ice Cream

● ● ● ● ● ●

Rocky Road Ice Cream comes in all different guises though always composed of chocolate (sometimes the ice cream and sometimes pieces), nuts, sometimes coconut and always and most notably marshmallows.

Although marshmallows are the most popular campfire treats, few people actually know what they are. Made by mixing corn syrup, powdered sugar, egg whites and unflavored gelatin, this mixture is then left to "harden" for about a day and then, traditionally, cut into bite-sized cubes. Before the invention of gelatin, an extract from the root of the marshmallow plant was used as a thickening agent. Hence the name. Today, marshmallows are known for their key role in s'mores as well as a popular topping for hot chocolate. For S'More Ice Cream: replace the pecans and coconut with 4 chopped graham crackers.

1 ½ cups whole milk

1 ½ cups heavy cream

½ cup white sugar

4 large egg yolks, at room temperature

1 teaspoon vanilla extract

Pinch kosher salt

¾ cup mini marshmallows, chopped if desired

½ cup chopped toasted pecans, walnuts or
   almonds

½ cup chopped chocolate chips

½ cup shredded sweetened coconut (optional)

Place the milk, cream and ¼ cup of the sugar in a small pan and cook over low heat, whisking from time to time, until it is warm, about 175°F.

Place the egg yolks, ¼ cup of the sugar, the vanilla extract and salt in a small metal bowl and whisk until completely mixed. Add ¼ cup of the warm milk mixture to the eggs, whisking all the while. Continue adding milk to the eggs, ¼ cup at a time, until you have added about 1½ cups. Slowly, whisking all the while, return the now milk and egg mixture to the remaining milk mixture in the pan and continue cooking until it just begins to thicken or reaches about 185°F. Do not allow the mixture to boil. Pour through a medium fine strainer into a metal bowl, discard the solids and set aside until it reaches room temperature.

continued on page 38

Cover and refrigerate until it reaches 40°F, about 3 hours. Transfer to an ice cream maker and proceed according to the manufacturer's instructions.

When the ice cream is just beginning to come together but has not hardened completely, add the marshmallows, pecans, chocolate chips and coconut, if desired, and process for about 5 more minutes.

German Chocolate Ice Cream

MAKES 1 1/2 TO 2 PINTS

I have taken all the flavors in German Chocolate Cake, one of my favorite cakes growing up, and adapted them to ice cream: chocolate, coconut and pecans. If you happen to have some leftover German Chocolate Cake, add it too!

1 1/2 cups whole milk	1 teaspoon vanilla extract
1 1/2 cups heavy cream	Pinch kosher salt
8 ounces German's chocolate, chopped	1 cup sweetened shredded coconut
2 egg yolks, at room temperature	1 cup lightly toasted chopped pecans

Place the milk, cream and chocolate in a small pan and cook over low heat, whisking from time to time, until it is warm, about 175°F.

Place the egg yolks, vanilla extract and salt in a small metal bowl and whisk until completely mixed. Add 1/4 cup of the warm milk mixture to the eggs, whisking all the while. Continue adding milk to the vanilla, 1/4 cup at a time, until you have added about 1 1/2 cups. Slowly, whisking all the while, return the now milk and egg mixture to the remaining milk mixture in the pan and continue cooking until it just begins to thicken or reaches about 185°F. Do not allow the mixture to boil. Pour through a medium fine strainer into a metal bowl, discard the solids and set aside until it reaches room temperature.

Cover and refrigerate until it reaches 40°F, about 3 hours. Transfer to an ice cream maker and proceed according to the manufacturer's instructions.

When the ice cream is just beginning to come together but has not hardened completely, add the coconut and pecans and process for about 5 more minutes.

Sour Cream Brown Sugar Ice Cream

MAKES 1 ½ TO 2 PINTS

When I was in high school my friend Emily Friedan and I used to buy strawberries from New York street vendors and then go home to dip them in brown sugar flecked sour cream. This childhood-inspired ice cream is very rich: be sure to use it as a dip for fresh strawberries.

1 ½ cups whole milk

½ cup heavy cream

6 tablespoons brown sugar

2 egg yolks, at room temperature

¾ teaspoon vanilla extract

Pinch kosher salt

1 cup sour cream

Place the milk, heavy cream and 2 tablespoons of the brown sugar in a small pan and cook over low heat, whisking from time to time, until it is warm, about 175°F.

Place the egg yolks, vanilla extract and salt in a small metal bowl and whisk until completely mixed. Add ¼ cup of the warm milk mixture to the eggs, whisking all the while. Continue adding milk to the egg mixture, ¼ cup at a time, until you have added about 1½ cups. Slowly, whisking all the while, return the now milk and egg mixture to the remaining milk mixture in the pan and continue cooking until it just begins to thicken or reaches about 185°F. Do not allow the mixture to boil. Pour through a medium fine strainer into a metal bowl, discard the solids and set aside until it reaches room temperature.

Add the sour cream and stir well. Cover and refrigerate until it reaches 40°F, about 3 hours. Transfer to an ice cream maker and proceed according to the manufacturer's instructions.

When the ice cream is just beginning to come together but has not hardened completely, add the remaining 4 tablespoons brown sugar, and process for about 5 more minutes. They will not dissolve: you want specks of brown sugar.

Avocado Gelato

● ● ● ● ● ● ● ● ●

MAKES 1 ½ TO 2 PINTS

Creamy, buttery, luscious and slightly nutty, a little bit of this unbelievably rich ice cream will intrigue and suffice. Garnish with toasted coconut, mint leaves, basil leaves and/or lightly toasted pistachios.

2 cups whole milk

1 cup heavy cream

¾ cup white sugar

5 perfectly ripe avocadoes, peeled, pitted and chopped

1 tablespoon fresh lime juice

1 teaspoon freshly grated lime zest (optional)

Pinch kosher salt

Place the milk, cream and sugar in a small pan and cook over low heat, whisking from time to time, until it is warm, about 175°F. Do not allow the mixture to boil. Set the mixture aside until it reaches room temperature.

Cover and refrigerate until it reaches 40°F, about 3 hours. Place the milk mixture, avocadoes, lime juice, lime zest, if desired, and salt in a blender and blend until smooth. Transfer to an ice cream maker and proceed according to the manufacturer's instructions.

Espresso Gelato with Biscotti

MAKES 1½ TO 2 PINTS

Having watched so many people dunk biscotti into their espresso, I was inspired to short-circuit the process and combine them in one intensely flavored ice cream.

2 cups whole milk

1 cup heavy cream

½ cup white sugar

¼ cup finely ground espresso coffee beans

2 large egg yolks, at room temperature

Pinch kosher salt

½ teaspoon vanilla extract

1 ½ cups crushed biscotti, plain or chocolate covered

Place the milk, cream, ¼ cup of the sugar and ground coffee beans in a small pan and cook over low heat, whisking from time to time, until it is warm, about 175°F.

Place the egg yolks, ¼ cup of the sugar and the salt in a small metal bowl and whisk until completely mixed. Add ¼ cup of the warm milk mixture to the eggs, whisking all the while. Continue adding milk to the eggs, ¼ cup at a time, until you have added about 1½ cups. Slowly, whisking all the while, return the now milk and egg mixture to the remaining milk mixture in the pan and continue cooking until it just begins to thicken or reaches about 185°F. Do not allow the mixture to boil. Set aside for 2 hours at room temperature. Pour through a medium fine strainer into a metal bowl and discard the solids.

Cover and refrigerate until it reaches 40°F, about 3 hours. Add the vanilla extract and stir well. Transfer to an ice cream maker and proceed according to the manufacturer's instructions.

When the ice cream is just beginning to come together but has not hardened completely, add the biscotti and process for about 5 more minutes.

Triple Coconut Ice Cream

● ● ● ● ●

I am a huge coconut enthusiast and this rendition—layer upon layer of coconut flavor— really packs it in. Add chopped dried apricots, chocolate chips or nuts or drizzle with Bittersweet Cocoa Sauce (see page 3).

1 cup whole milk	Pinch kosher salt
1 cup heavy cream	1 teaspoon vanilla extract
1 cup coconut milk	¼ cup shredded sweetened coconut
½ cup white sugar	½ cup toasted, shredded sweetened coconut
2 large egg yolks, at room temperature	(see page xii)

Place the milk, cream, coconut milk and ¼ cup of the sugar in a small pan and cook over low heat, whisking from time to time, until it is warm, about 175°F.

Place the egg yolks, ¼ cup of the sugar and the salt in a small metal bowl and whisk until completely mixed. Add ¼ cup of the warm milk mixture to the eggs, whisking all the while. Continue adding milk to the eggs, ¼ cup at a time, until you have added about 1½ cups. Slowly, whisking all the while, return the now milk and egg mixture to the remaining milk mixture in the pan and continue cooking until it just begins to thicken or reaches about 185°F. Do not allow the mixture to boil. Pour through a medium fine strainer into a metal bowl, discard the solids and set aside until it reaches room temperature.

Add the vanilla extract and stir to combine. Cover and refrigerate until it reaches 40°F, about 3 hours. Transfer to an ice cream maker and proceed according to the manufacturer's instructions.

When the ice cream is just beginning to come together but has not hardened completely, add the coconut and process for about 5 more minutes.

Fresh Peach & Marcona Almond Gelato

More subtle, sweeter and juicier than your standard almond, Spanish Marcona almonds are hands down my favorite nut. Available raw or in sunflower oil and sea salt, it's the latter ones that get my attention for both eating and cooking. Make this ice cream during the summer when peaches are at their best: the combination of the sweet juicy peach and the firm, slightly salty almond is breathtaking. This ice cream takes forever to freeze so don't bother waiting—when it is close, just finish the process in the freezer.

4 ¼ cups pitted, skinned and diced peaches

2 cups whole milk

1 cup heavy cream

4 large egg yolks, at room temperature

½ cup white sugar

Pinch kosher salt

2 teaspoons fresh lemon juice

½ teaspoon vanilla extract

1 cup Marcona almonds, coarsely chopped

Place the peaches in a shallow bowl, cover and set aside at room temperature for at least 2 hours and up to overnight. From time to time, mash with a potato masher, until the peaches are completely broken up but still have some texture. Cover and refrigerate at least 1 hour.

In the meantime, place the milk and cream in a small pan and cook over low heat, whisking from time to time, until it is warm, about 175°F.

Place the egg yolks, ¼ cup of the sugar and the salt in a small metal bowl and whisk until completely mixed. Add ¼ cup of the warm milk mixture to the eggs, whisking all the while. Continue adding milk to the eggs, ¼ cup at a time, until you have added about 1½ cups. Slowly, whisking all the while, return the now milk and egg mixture to the remaining milk mixture in the pan and continue cooking until it just begins to thicken or reaches about 185°F. Do not allow the mixture to boil. Pour through a medium fine strainer into a metal bowl, discard the solids and set aside until it reaches room temperature.

Add the peaches, lemon juice and vanilla extract and stir well. Cover and refrigerate until it reaches 40°F, about 3 hours. Transfer to an ice cream maker and proceed according to the manufacturer's instructions.

When the ice cream is just beginning to come together but has not hardened completely, add the almonds and process for about 5 more minutes.

Gingered Ginger Ice Cream

MAKES 1½ TO 2 PINTS

Spicy, pungent, aromatic, this ice cream is so gingery it almost hurts. Leftover gingerbread is a heady addition.

1½ cups whole milk	½ cup white sugar
1½ cups heavy cream	4 large egg yolks, at room temperature
½ cup fresh ginger root, peeled and finely chopped	1 teaspoon vanilla extract
	Pinch kosher salt
1 teaspoon ground ginger	¼ cup candied ginger, finely chopped (optional)

Place the milk, cream, ginger root, ground ginger and ¼ cup of the sugar in a small pan and cook over low heat, whisking from time to time, until it is warm, about 175°F. Set aside for 1 hour. Pour through a medium strainer into a metal bowl, reserving 2 tablespoons ginger root for later. Discard the rest.

Place the egg yolks, ¼ cup of the sugar, the vanilla extract and salt in a small metal bowl and whisk until completely mixed. Add ¼ cup of the warm milk mixture to the eggs, whisking all the while. Continue adding milk to the eggs, ¼ cup at a time, until you have added about 1½ cups. Slowly, whisking all the while, return the now milk and egg mixture to the remaining milk mixture in the pan and continue cooking until it just begins to thicken or reaches about 185°F. Do not allow the mixture to boil. Pour through a medium fine strainer into a metal bowl, discard the solids and set aside until it reaches room temperature.

Cover and refrigerate until it reaches 40°F, about 3 hours. Return 2 tablespoons ginger root to the mixture, stir to combine and transfer to an ice cream maker and proceed according to the manufacturer's instructions.

When the ice cream is just beginning to come together but has not hardened completely, add the candied ginger, if desired, and process for about 5 more minutes.

Cookie Dough Ice Cream

MAKES 1 ½ TO 2 PINTS

Chocolate chip cookie dough is the classic choice, but you can use anything you like: in fact you should probably buy my cookie book, *Recipe of the Week: Cookies*, and make your selection from the fifty-two options. You can use pasteurized egg substitute in the cookie dough, if you're concerned about the risk of eating raw eggs.

1 ½ cups whole milk

1 ½ cups heavy cream

¼ cup sugar syrup (see page xiii) or white sugar

1 teaspoon vanilla extract

1 ½ cups of your favorite raw cookie dough, such as chocolate chip or oatmeal

If using sugar syrup: Place the milk, cream, sugar syrup and vanilla extract in a bowl and whisk well. Transfer to an ice cream maker and proceed according to the manufacturer's instructions.

If using sugar: Place the milk, cream and sugar in a small pan and cook over low heat, whisking from time to time, until it is warm, about 175°F. Do not allow the mixture to boil. Set the mixture aside until it reaches room temperature. Cover and refrigerate until it reaches 40°F, about 3 hours. Add the vanilla, transfer to an ice cream maker and proceed according to the manufacturer's instructions.

When the ice cream is just beginning to come together but has not hardened completely, add spoonfuls of the cookie dough and process for about 5 more minutes.

Oreo® Ice Cream

MAKES 1½ TO 2 PINTS

Milk and cookies don't get any more classic or homey than this. In order to get the consistency of cookies dunked in milk, add the Oreos just before the ice cream is finished so they don't become soggy. Unless of course you like it that way, in which case add them the same time you add the cream.

1 ½ cups whole milk	1 teaspoon vanilla extract
1 ½ cups heavy cream	1 ½ cups crushed Oreo cookies (with the
¼ cup sugar syrup (see page xiii) or white	cream filling scraped off)
sugar	

If using sugar syrup: Place the milk, cream, sugar syrup and vanilla extract in a bowl and whisk well. Transfer to an ice cream maker and proceed according to the manufacturer's instructions.

If using sugar: Place the milk, cream and sugar in a small pan and cook over low heat, whisking from time to time, until it is warm, about 175°F. Do not allow the mixture to boil. Set the mixture aside until it reaches room temperature. Cover and refrigerate until it reaches 40°F, about 3 hours. Add the vanilla, transfer to an ice cream maker and proceed according to the manufacturer's instructions.

When the ice cream is just beginning to come together but has not hardened completely, add the Oreos and process for about 5 more minutes.

Coffee Gelato

Real coffee beans—my favorite is half French roast and half Sumatra—infused in the milk-cream-sugar mixture impart the best coffee flavor, but if you must, instant is certainly acceptable.

2 cups whole milk

1 cup heavy cream

½ cup white sugar

¼ cup finely ground coffee beans

⅓ cup very coarsely ground coffee beans

4 large egg yolks, at room temperature

Pinch kosher salt

2 teaspoons vanilla extract

Place the milk, cream, ¼ cup of the sugar and the ground coffee beans in a small pan and cook over low heat, whisking from time to time, until it is warm, about 175°F.

Place the egg yolks, ¼ cup of the sugar and the salt in a small metal bowl and whisk until completely mixed. Add ¼ cup of the warm milk mixture to the eggs, whisking all the while. Continue adding milk to the eggs, ¼ cup at a time, until you have added about 1½ cups. Slowly, whisking all the while, return the now milk and egg mixture to the remaining milk mixture in the pan and continue cooking until it just begins to thicken or reaches about 185°F. Do not allow the mixture to boil. Set aside for 2 hours at room temperature. Pour through a medium fine strainer into a metal bowl and discard the solids.

Cover and refrigerate until it reaches 40°F, about 3 hours. Add the vanilla extract and stir well. Transfer to an ice cream maker and proceed according to the manufacturer's instructions.

Burnt Caramel Gelato

Although I wasn't the first to discover this flavor (by a long shot), like everyone else I discovered it by making a mistake and almost burning caramel. The toastiness of the caramel is just amazing. If you like this flavor, you will probably become—as most people do—obsessed with it.

¾ cup white sugar

1 tablespoon water

1 cup heavy cream

2 cups whole milk

4 large egg yolks, at room temperature

1 teaspoon vanilla extract

¼ teaspoon kosher salt

Place the sugar and water in a pan and bring to a boil. Continue boiling, without stirring, until it turns a deep brown and begins to smell toasty, 2 to 3 minutes. Slowly and very carefully add the cream. Continue whisking until the cream is incorporated. Slowly, add the milk and cook over low heat, whisking from time to time, until it is warm, about 175°F. Add the vanilla extract and salt.

Place the egg yolks in a small metal bowl and whisk until completely mixed. Add ¼ cup of the warm milk mixture to the eggs, whisking all the while. Continue adding milk to the eggs, ¼ cup at a time, until you have added about 1½ cups. Slowly, whisking all the while, return the now milk and egg mixture to the remaining milk mixture in the pan and continue cooking until it just begins to thicken or reaches about 185°F. Do not allow the mixture to boil. Pour through a medium fine strainer into a metal bowl, discard the solids and set aside until it reaches room temperature.

Cover and refrigerate until it reaches 40°F, about 3 hours. Transfer to an ice cream maker and proceed according to the manufacturer's instructions.

Dark Chocolate Gelato with Cranberries and Nuts

MAKES 1 ½ TO 2 PINTS

This recipe calls for a large quantity of mix-ins, which makes the ice cream kind of craggy and wild, which is just what I am looking for. The contrast of the almost wine-like semi-sweet chocolate, tart cranberries, salty nuts and creamy white chocolate with the cold, luscious ice cream is absolutely wicked.

2 cups whole milk

1 cup heavy cream

8 ounces semi-sweet chocolate

2 tablespoons white sugar

1 teaspoon vanilla extract

1 cup chopped dried cranberries

1 cup chopped toasted lightly salted almonds, walnuts or pecans

1 cup chopped white chocolate

Place the milk, cream, chocolate and sugar in a small pan and cook over low heat, whisking from time to time, until the chocolate has dissolved and the mixture is warm, about 175°F. Do not allow the mixture to boil. Set the mixture aside until it reaches room temperature.

Cover and refrigerate until it reaches 40°F, about 3 hours. Add the vanilla extract, transfer to an ice cream maker and proceed according to the manufacturer's instructions.

When the ice cream is just beginning to come together but has not hardened completely, add the cranberries, almonds and white chocolate and process for about 5 more minutes.

Cinnamon Stick Ice Cream

MAKES 1½ TO 2 PINTS

Warm, fragrant and just sweet, ground cinnamon and cinnamon stick come from the same plant but have very different culinary uses. Ground cinnamon, the most commonly used baking spice, is best used as a flavoring ingredient for pies, cakes and other solid foods. It can also be used in rubs for savory foods. Cinnamon stick, made from rolled, dried pieces of bark, is best used in hot drinks, where its more delicate flavor is extracted over long periods of time. Using both in ice cream gets the best results. Serve with fresh berries.

1 ½ cups whole milk

1 ½ cups heavy cream

½ cup white sugar

1 cinnamon stick

¼ teaspoon ground cinnamon

6 large egg yolks, at room temperature

Pinch kosher salt

Place the milk, cream, ¼ cup of the sugar, the cinnamon stick and ground cinnamon in a small pan and cook over low heat, whisking from time to time, until it is warm, about 175°F.

Place the egg yolks, ¼ cup of the sugar and the salt in a small metal bowl and whisk until completely mixed. Add ¼ cup of the warm milk mixture to the eggs, whisking all the while. Continue adding milk to the eggs, ¼ cup at a time, until you have added about 1½ cups. Slowly, whisking all the while, return the now milk and egg mixture to the remaining milk mixture in the pan and continue cooking until it just begins to thicken or reaches about 185°F. Do not allow the mixture to boil. Set the mixture aside until it reaches room temperature.

Cover and refrigerate until it reaches 40°F, about 3 hours. Pour through a medium fine strainer into a metal bowl and discard the solids, including the cinnamon stick. Transfer to an ice cream maker and proceed according to the manufacturer's instructions.

Grape-Nuts® Ice Cream

MAKES 1½ TO 2 PINTS

Nutty, crunchy and malty, Grape-Nuts is one of my favorite cereals and yet the first time I was offered this ice cream I politely declined. This combination seemed too bizarre, even for me, although it's hugely popular in New England, where we live. After my son, Ben, kept ordering it I felt I was obligated to try it, and eureka! I found it completely captivating.

1 ½ cups whole milk

1 ½ cups heavy cream

⅓ cup white sugar

2 large egg yolks, at room temperature

1 teaspoon vanilla extract

1 ½ cups Grape-Nuts

¾ cup raisins, currants, dried cranberries
    or dried cherries (optional)

Place the milk, cream and sugar in a small pan and cook over low heat, whisking from time to time, until it is warm, about 175°F.

Place the egg yolks and vanilla extract in a small metal bowl and whisk until completely mixed. Add ¼ cup of the warm milk mixture to the eggs, whisking all the while. Continue adding milk to the eggs, ¼ cup at a time, until you have added about 1½ cups. Slowly, whisking all the while, return the now milk and egg mixture to the remaining milk mixture in the pan and continue cooking until it just begins to thicken or reaches about 185°F. Do not allow the mixture to boil. Pour through a medium fine strainer into a metal bowl, discard the solids and set aside until it reaches room temperature.

Cover and refrigerate until it reaches 40°F, about 3 hours. Transfer to an ice cream maker and proceed according to the manufacturer's instructions.

When the ice cream is just beginning to come together but has not hardened completely, add the Grape-Nuts and the dried fruit, if desired, and process for about 5 more minutes.

Molasses Ginger Snap Gelato

MAKES 1 ½ TO 2 PINTS

My childhood friend Lizzy Shaw will be so happy to see this recipe: on scores of her yearly trips to Boston, she has been known to pack a few quarts in ice and take it home with her to LA.

2 cups whole milk

1 cup heavy cream

¼ cup dark molasses

2 large egg yolks, at room temperature

2 tablespoons white sugar or sugar syrup
   (see page xiii)

½ teaspoon vanilla extract

Pinch kosher salt

8 ginger snaps, store-bought or homemade,
   crumbled (about 2 cups)

Place the milk, cream and molasses in a small pan and cook over low heat, whisking from time to time, until it is warm, about 175°F.

Place the egg yolks, sugar, vanilla extract and salt in a small metal bowl and whisk until completely mixed. Add ¼ cup of the warm milk mixture to the eggs, whisking all the while. Continue adding milk to the eggs, ¼ cup at a time, until you have added about 1½ cups. Slowly, whisking all the while, return the now milk and egg mixture to the remaining milk mixture in the pan and continue cooking until it just begins to thicken or reaches about 185°F. Do not allow the mixture to boil. Pour through a medium fine strainer into a metal bowl, discard the solids and set aside until it reaches room temperature.

Cover and refrigerate until it reaches 40°F, about 3 hours. Transfer to an ice cream maker and proceed according to the manufacturer's instructions.

When the ice cream is just beginning to come together but has not hardened completely, add the ginger snaps and process for about 5 more minutes.

Rhubarberry Ice Cream with Crisp Topping

MAKES 1½ TO 2 PINTS

When I was making this ice cream, my son, Ben, walked into the house and assumed I was making a Blueberry Rhubarb Crisp, one of his favorite desserts. It gave me the idea to serve the ice cream with the topping I use on crisps. When my daughter, Lauren, smelled the topping she suggested I add it when still hot to the cold ice cream. A great meeting of the minds!

FOR THE ICE CREAM:

2 cups sliced fresh rhubarb stalks

1 cup fresh blueberries

½ cup white sugar

1 teaspoon lemon juice

2 cups half and half

2 large egg yolks, at room temperature

Pinch kosher salt

FOR THE TOPPING:

¼ cup (½ stick) unsalted butter, melted

1 tablespoon white sugar

1 teaspoon brown sugar

⅓ cup all-purpose flour

⅓ cup old-fashioned oats

¼ cup chopped pecans or walnuts

Pinch kosher salt

To make the ice cream: Place the rhubarb, blueberries and ¼ cup of the sugar in a medium size pan and cook over low heat until the fruit has softened and is bubbling, about 4 minutes. Set aside to cool to room temperature, add the lemon juice and stir well. Cover and refrigerate.

Place the half and half in a small pan and cook over low heat, whisking from time to time, until it is warm, about 175°F.

Place the egg yolks, ¼ cup of the sugar and the salt in a small metal bowl and whisk until completely mixed. Add ¼ cup of the warm half and half to the eggs, whisking all the while. Continue adding half and half to the eggs, ¼ cup at a time, until you have added about 1½ cups. Slowly, whisking all the while, return the now half and half and egg mixture to the remaining half and half in the pan and continue cooking until it just begins to thicken or reaches about 185°F. Do not allow the mixture to boil. Pour through a medium fine strainer into a metal bowl, discard the solids and set aside until it reaches room temperature. Add the chilled rhubarb mixture and combine well.

Cover and refrigerate until it reaches 40°F, about 3 hours. Transfer to an ice cream maker and proceed according to the manufacturer's instructions.

To make the topping: Preheat the oven to 350°F.

Place all the topping ingredients in a small bowl, toss well and transfer to a baking sheet. Bake until lightly toasted, about 20 minutes. Serve warm or at room temperature, sprinkled on top of the ice cream.

Nutmeg Ice Cream

MAKES 1 ½ TO 2 PINTS

The only way to make this slightly warm-spicy, sweet, almost nutty ice cream is to use fresh nutmeg and grate it yourself. Fresh nutmeg is readily available at specialty and spice shops. Ground nutmeg just won't do.

1 ½ cups whole milk

1 ½ cups heavy cream

½ cup brown sugar

1 ½ teaspoons freshly grated nutmeg

¼ teaspoon ground cinnamon

¼ teaspoon ground ginger

4 large egg yolks, at room temperature

Pinch kosher salt

1 teaspoon vanilla extract

1 cup chopped raisins (optional)

Place the milk, cream, ¼ cup of the brown sugar, nutmeg, cinnamon and ginger in a small pan and cook over low heat, whisking from time to time, until it is warm, about 175°F.

Place the egg yolks, ¼ cup of the brown sugar and the salt in a small metal bowl and whisk until completely mixed. Add ¼ cup of the warm milk mixture to the eggs, whisking all the while. Continue adding milk to the eggs, ¼ cup at a time, until you have added about 1½ cups. Slowly, whisking all the while, return the now milk and egg mixture to the remaining milk mixture in the pan and continue cooking until it just begins to thicken or reaches about 185°F. Do not allow the mixture to boil. Pour through a medium fine strainer into a metal bowl, discard the solids and set aside until it reaches room temperature. Add the vanilla extract and stir well.

Cover and refrigerate until it reaches 40°F, about 3 hours. Transfer to an ice cream maker and proceed according to the manufacturer's instructions.

When the ice cream is just beginning to come together but has not hardened completely, add the raisins, if desired, and process for about 5 more minutes.

Basil Gelato

Although basil is most known for its use in pesto, this clean and refreshing ice cream is not as outlandish as it sounds. Really. Plus it's stunningly beautiful.

2 cups whole milk

1 cup heavy cream

½ cup white sugar

4 large egg yolks, at room temperature

Pinch kosher salt

½ cup finely chopped fresh basil leaves

Place the milk, cream and ¼ cup of the sugar in a small pan and cook over low heat, whisking from time to time, until it is warm, about 175°F.

Place the egg yolks, ¼ cup of the sugar and the salt in a small metal bowl and whisk until completely mixed. Add ¼ cup of the warm milk mixture to the eggs, whisking all the while. Continue adding milk to the eggs, ¼ cup at a time, until you have added about 1½ cups. Slowly, whisking all the while, return the now milk and egg mixture to the remaining milk mixture in the pan and continue cooking until it just begins to thicken or reaches about 185°F. Do not allow the mixture to boil. Pour through a medium fine strainer into a metal bowl, discard the solids and set aside until it reaches room temperature.

Cover and refrigerate until it reaches 40°F, about 3 hours. Add the basil leaves and stir to combine. Transfer to an ice cream maker and proceed according to the manufacturer's instructions.

Pumpkin Gelato

When I was in college there was a—now defunct—ice cream shop that made the most irresistible pumpkin ice cream. After initially turning up his nose, my son Ben described it as cold pumpkin pie without the crust, which led us to another idea: fill a crust with this ice cream and then you really have cold pumpkin ice cream pie. Garnish with toasted or spiced pecans.

2 cups whole milk

1 cup heavy cream

½ cup brown sugar

1 teaspoon ground cinnamon

½ teaspoon ground ginger

⅛ teaspoon ground nutmeg

⅛ teaspoon ground allspice

1 large egg yolk, at room temperature

Pinch kosher salt

1 cup canned unsweetened pumpkin puree

1 teaspoon vanilla extract

2 tablespoons bourbon (optional)

Place the milk, cream, ¼ cup of the brown sugar, cinnamon, ginger, nutmeg and all-spice in a small pan and cook over low heat, whisking from time to time, until it is warm, about 175°F.

Place the egg yolk, ¼ cup of the brown sugar and the salt in a small metal bowl and whisk until completely mixed. Add ¼ cup of the warm milk mixture to the egg, whisking all the while. Continue adding milk to the egg, ¼ cup at a time, until you have added about 1½ cups. Slowly, whisking all the while, return the now milk and egg mixture to the remaining milk mixture in the pan and continue cooking until it just begins to thicken or reaches about 185°F. Do not allow the mixture to boil. Set the mixture aside until it reaches room temperature. Pour through a medium fine strainer into a metal bowl and discard the solids. Add the pumpkin, vanilla extract and bourbon, if desired, and mix well.

Cover and refrigerate until it reaches 40°F, about 3 hours. Transfer to an ice cream maker and proceed according to the manufacturer's instructions.

Mango Ice Cream

Though it's tempting to use fresh mango for this ice cream the truth is that canned puree offers better and certainly more consistent results. It is, of course, also less time consuming and less messy and as long as you have access to an Indian food shop, it employs ingredients that with a little planning, can readily be on hand. Good additions include toasted almonds, fresh or toasted coconut and fresh or frozen raspberries.

3 cups half and half	Pinch kosher salt
½ cup white sugar	1 ½ cups canned mango puree
1 large egg yolk, at room temperature	2 tablespoons fresh lemon or lime juice

Place the half and half and ¼ cup of the sugar in a small pan and cook over low heat, whisking from time to time, until it is warm, about 175°F.

Place the egg yolk, ¼ cup of the sugar and the salt in a small metal bowl and whisk until completely mixed. Add ¼ cup of the warm milk mixture to the egg, whisking all the while. Continue adding milk to the egg, ¼ cup at a time, until you have added about 1½ cups. Slowly, whisking all the while, return the now milk and egg mixture to the remaining milk mixture in the pan and continue cooking until it just begins to thicken or reaches about 185°F. Do not allow the mixture to boil. Set the mixture aside until it reaches room temperature. Pour through a medium fine strainer into a metal bowl and discard the solids. Add the mango puree and lemon juice and mix well.

Cover and refrigerate until it reaches 40°F, about 3 hours. Transfer to an ice cream maker and proceed according to the manufacturer's instructions.

Licorice Fennel Ice Cream

MAKES 1 1/2 TO 2 PINTS

I am a big fan of licorice and was inspired to make this because I had some in my pantry. The addition of the dried fennel and the Sambuca makes this ice cream a real treat for anyone who likes the sweet-bitter-warm flavor of licorice. And yet, with all the layers of licorice, the flavor is surprisingly subtle.

3 cups half and half	Pinch kosher salt
1/2 cup white sugar	2 tablespoons Sambuca
2 teaspoons dried fennel seed, lightly toasted and finely ground	12 pieces good quality black licorice, finely chopped
3 large egg yolks, at room temperature	

Place the half and half, 1/4 cup of the sugar and fennel seed in a small pan and cook over low heat, whisking from time to time, until it is warm, about 175°F.

Place the egg yolks, 1/4 cup of the sugar and the salt in a small metal bowl and whisk until completely mixed. Add 1/4 cup of the warm half and half mixture to the eggs, whisking all the while. Continue adding half and half to the eggs, 1/4 cup at a time, until you have added about 1 1/2 cups. Slowly, whisking all the while, return the now half and half and egg mixture to the remaining half and half mixture in the pan and continue cooking until it just begins to thicken or reaches about 185°F. Do not allow the mixture to boil. Set the mixture aside until it reaches room temperature. Pour through a medium fine strainer into a metal bowl and discard the solids. Add the Sambuca and stir well.

Cover and refrigerate until it reaches 40°F, about 3 hours. Transfer to an ice cream maker and proceed according to the manufacturer's instructions.

When the ice cream is just beginning to come together but has not hardened completely, add the licorice and process for about 5 more minutes.

Strawberry Gelato

MAKES 1 ½ TO 2 PINTS

Strawberry ice cream is considered to be one of the hardest flavors to get right: it's almost impossible to get a lot of strawberry flavor without having huge rocks of frozen strawberries throughout. This gelato has about twice the strawberries as most recipes and not a rock in sight!

3 cups diced, hulled fresh strawberries	4 large egg yolks, at room temperature
¾ cup white sugar	Pinch kosher salt
2 cups whole milk	2 teaspoons fresh lemon or lime juice
1 cup heavy cream	1 teaspoon vanilla extract

Before you start making the ice cream: Place the strawberries and ½ cup of the sugar in a bowl and set aside at room temperature for at least 2 hours and up to overnight. From time to time, mash with a potato masher, until the berries are completely broken up. Cover and refrigerate at least 1 hour and up to 2 hours.

Place the milk and cream in a small pan and cook over low heat, whisking from time to time, until it is warm, about 175°F.

Place the egg yolks, ¼ cup of the sugar and the salt in a small metal bowl and whisk until completely mixed. Add ¼ cup of the warm milk mixture to the eggs, whisking all the while. Continue adding milk to the eggs, ¼ cup at a time, until you have added about 1½ cups. Slowly, whisking all the while, return the now milk and egg mixture to the remaining milk mixture in the pan and continue cooking until it just begins to thicken or reaches about 185°F. Do not allow the mixture to boil. Pour through a medium fine strainer into a metal bowl, discard the solids and set aside until it reaches room temperature.

Add the reserved strawberries, lemon juice and vanilla extract to the milk mixture and stir well. Cover and refrigerate until it reaches 40°F, about 3 hours. Transfer to an ice cream maker and proceed according to the manufacturer's instructions.

Banana Ice Cream with Burnt Caramel Sauce

MAKES 1 ½ TO 2 PINTS

The intriguing combination of the bananas, rum and burnt caramel will transport you to a Caribbean island. Garnish with toasted almonds or pecans, fresh or chopped dried apricots, blueberries, shaved chocolate or strawberries.

FOR THE ICE CREAM:

3 cups half and half

2 large egg yolks, at room temperature

2 tablespoons brown sugar

Pinch kosher salt

3 overripe bananas, pureed

2 teaspoons rum or fresh lemon juice

FOR THE BURNT CARAMEL SAUCE:

¾ cup white sugar

1 tablespoon water

1 cup heavy cream

1 teaspoon vanilla extract

¼ teaspoon kosher salt

To make the ice cream: Place the half and half in a small pan and cook over low heat, whisking from time to time, until it is warm, about 175°F.

Place the egg yolks, brown sugar and salt in a small metal bowl and whisk until completely mixed. Add ¼ cup of the warm half and half mixture to the eggs, whisking all the while. Continue adding half and half to the eggs, ¼ cup at a time, until you have added about 1½ cups. Slowly, whisking all the while, return the now half and half and egg mixture to the remaining milk mixture in the pan and continue cooking until it just begins to thicken or reaches about 185°F. Do not allow the mixture to boil. Pour through a medium fine strainer into a metal bowl, discard the solids and set aside until it reaches room temperature. Add the bananas and rum and mix well.

Cover and refrigerate until it reaches 40°F, about 3 hours. Transfer to an ice cream maker and proceed according to the manufacturer's instructions.

To make the burnt caramel sauce: Place the sugar and water in a pot and bring to

continued on page 74

a boil. Continue boiling, without stirring, until it begins to color on the edges, about 2 to 3 minutes. Cook, whisking all the while, until it turns a deep brown and just begins to smell burnt, 3 to 4 minutes. Slowly and very carefully add the cream, continuing to whisk, until it is completely incorporated. Off heat, add the vanilla and salt. Serve immediately or cool to room temperature, cover and refrigerate.

Coconut Apricot Sorbet

Often used interchangeably on menus, there is actually a big difference between sorbet and sherbet (aka sherbert). Sorbet is made from iced fruit juice or puree and contains no milk, no cream and no eggs. Aside from being eaten as a dessert, sorbet is often served as a palate cleanser between courses. Sherbet is a cross between ice cream and sorbet: essentially a form of sorbet that contains milk and eggs. It is often served as a lower fat alternative to ice cream.

½ cup white sugar

½ cup boiling water

2 cups unsweetened coconut milk

2 cups unsweetened apricot juice

1 cup unsweetened coconut flakes

Place the sugar and boiling water in a medium bowl and stir until the sugar has dissolved. Add the coconut milk and apricot juice and stir to combine. Cover and refrigerate until it reaches 40°F, about 3 hours. Add the coconut and stir well. Transfer to an ice cream maker and proceed according to the manufacturer's instructions.

Green Tea Gelato

Considered one of the most beneficial natural supplements, green tea has become widely popularized in the United States. Its subtle taste and almost rich texture make it perfect for ice cream. Touted for its health benefits, it is thought to help with headaches, indigestion and the risk of heart disease. With its high amounts of antioxidants, it protects against free radicals, which helps boost the immune system, so . . . who says ice cream isn't nutritious?

2 cups whole milk

1 cup heavy cream

2 tablespoons powdered green tea (also called matcha and available at specialty and tea shops)

½ cup white sugar

4 large egg yolks, at room temperature

Pinch kosher salt

Place the milk, cream, powdered green tea and ¼ cup of the sugar in a small pan and cook over low heat, whisking from time to time, until it is warm, about 175°F.

Place the egg yolks, ¼ cup of the sugar and the salt in a small metal bowl and whisk until completely mixed. Add ¼ cup of the warm milk mixture to the eggs, whisking all the while. Continue adding milk to the eggs, ¼ cup at a time, until you have added about 1½ cups. Slowly, whisking all the while, return the now milk and egg mixture to the remaining milk mixture in the pan and continue cooking until it just begins to thicken or reaches about 185°F. Do not allow the mixture to boil. Pour through a medium fine strainer into a metal bowl, discard the solids and set aside until it reaches room temperature.

Cover and refrigerate until it reaches 40°F, about 3 hours. Transfer to an ice cream maker and proceed according to the manufacturer's instructions.

Orange Pineapple Coconut Sorbet

MAKES 1 ¹/₂ TO 2 PINTS

Don't be confused by the coconut milk: there isn't a bit of dairy in this.

1 cup fresh orange juice

1 cup pineapple juice

1 cup coconut milk

Place the orange and pineapple juices and coconut milk in a bowl and whisk until mixed well. Cover and refrigerate until the mixture reaches 40°F.

Transfer to an ice cream maker and proceed according to the manufacturer's instructions.

Cranberry Lime Sorbet

MAKES 1 ½ TO 2 PINTS

Brilliant pastry chef Paige Retus taught me how to make this wonderfully tart sorbet without the aid of an ice cream machine. I have been making it for years and years for all sorts of occasions, but without fail at Thanksgiving. I didn't know it could be improved upon, but the texture is even better with an ice cream machine. I like to serve this with dark chocolate cookies.

1 cup white sugar

2 ½ cups water

2 ½ cups cranberries, picked over for leaves

¾ cup fresh lime juice or orange juice

Zest of 1 lime

Place the sugar and 1 cup of the water in a small saucepan and bring to a boil over high heat. When the sugar has dissolved, add the cranberries and return to a boil. Cook until the cranberries pop, about 4 minutes. Set aside to cool. Place in a blender and puree until smooth.

Add the remaining 1½ cups water, lime juice and lime zest to the blender and puree. Cover and refrigerate until the mixture reaches 40°F. Transfer to an ice cream maker and proceed according to the manufacturer's instructions.

Toasted Pecan Gelato

MAKES 1 1/2 TO 2 PINTS

This gelato is my true favorite and the only item in the book I wasn't able to resist eating and eating and eating. I would have a scoop, and put the rest back in the freezer only to return again for another scoop. And on and on until it was all gone.

2 cups whole milk

1 cup heavy cream

2/3 cup light brown sugar

4 large egg yolks, at room temperature

Pinch kosher salt

1 cup toasted pecans (see page xii), finely ground

1/2 teaspoon vanilla extract

Place the milk, cream and 1/3 cup of the brown sugar in a small pan and cook over low heat, whisking from time to time, until it is warm, about 175°F.

Place the egg yolks, 1/3 cup of the brown sugar and salt in a small metal bowl and whisk until completely mixed. Add 1/4 cup of the warm milk mixture to the eggs, whisking all the while. Continue adding milk to the eggs, 1/4 cup at a time, until you have added about 1 1/2 cups. Slowly, whisking all the while, return the now milk and egg mixture to the remaining milk mixture in the pan and continue cooking until it just begins to thicken or reaches about 185°F. Do not allow the mixture to boil. Pour through a medium fine strainer into a metal bowl. Discard the solids. Add the pecans and stir well. Set the mixture aside until it reaches room temperature. Add the vanilla extract and stir well.

Cover and refrigerate until it reaches 40°F, about 3 hours. Transfer to an ice cream maker and proceed according to the manufacturer's instructions.

Cranberry Gelato

Cranberry lovers will flip for this gelato: it is at once creamy and rich like ice cream but tart and fruity like sorbet.

2 cups whole milk	Pinch kosher salt
1 cup heavy cream	½ cup cranberry concentrate or unsweetened
½ cup white sugar	cranberry juice
4 large egg yolks, at room temperature	½ teaspoon vanilla extract

Place the milk, cream and ¼ cup of the sugar in a small pan and cook over low heat, whisking from time to time, until it is warm, about 175°F.

Place the egg yolks, ¼ cup of the sugar and the salt in a small metal bowl and whisk until completely mixed. Add ¼ cup of the warm milk mixture to the eggs, whisking all the while. Continue adding milk to the eggs, ¼ cup at a time, until you have added about 1½ cups. Slowly, whisking all the while, return the now milk and egg mixture to the remaining milk mixture in the pan and continue cooking until it just begins to thicken or reaches about 185°F. Do not allow the mixture to boil. Pour through a medium fine strainer into a metal bowl. Discard the solids. Add the cranberry concentrate and vanilla extract and stir well. Set the mixture aside until it reaches room temperature.

Cover and refrigerate until it reaches 40°F, about 3 hours. Transfer to an ice cream maker and proceed according to the manufacturer's instructions.

list of recipe titles by the week

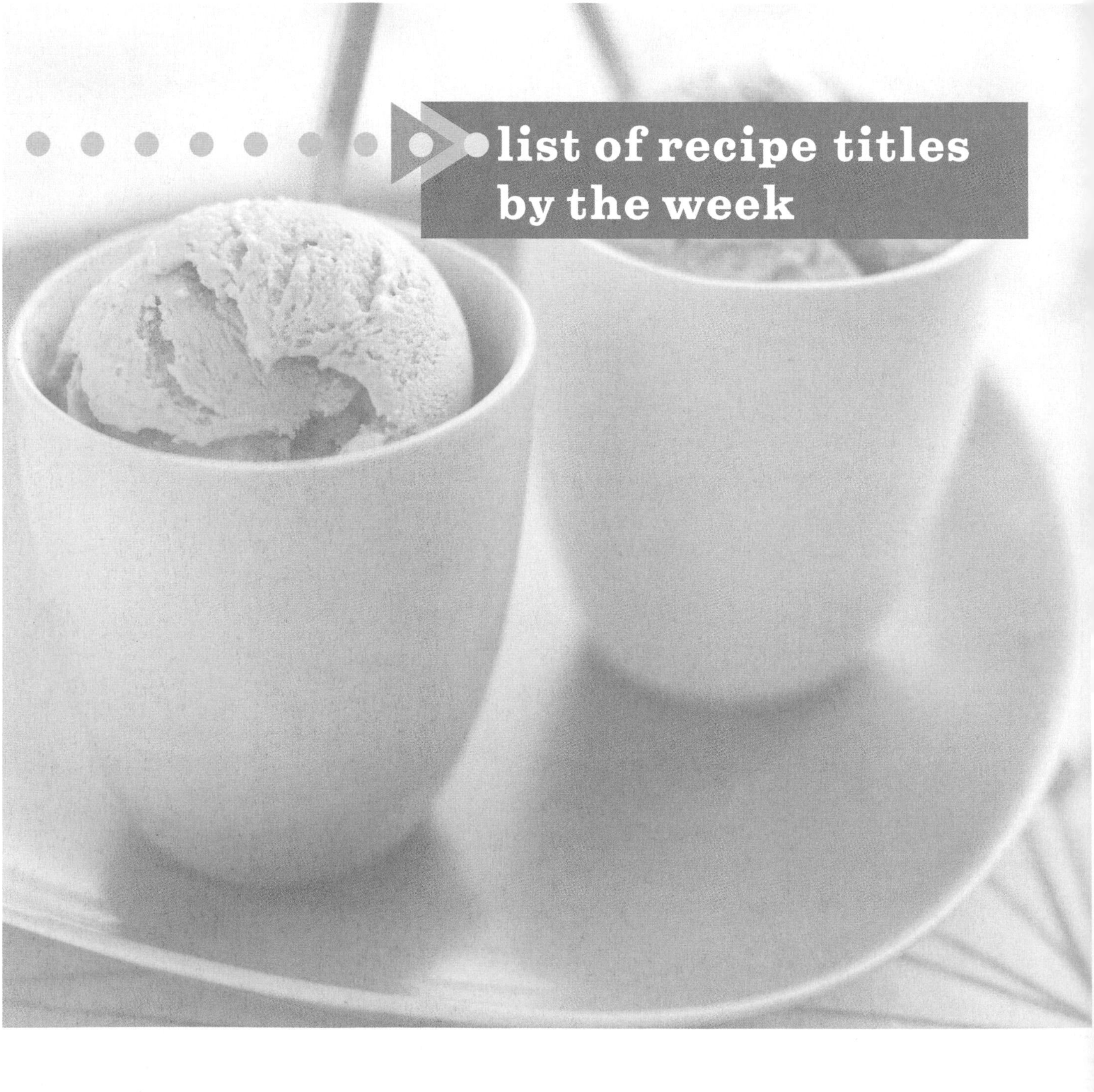

ICE CREAM

Index